W9-ADX-217

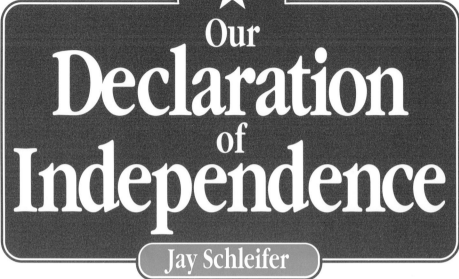

Our
Declaration
of
Independence

Jay Schleifer

THE MILLBROOK PRESS
Brookfield, Connecticut

Published by The Millbrook Press
2 Old New Milford Road
Brookfield, CT 06804
© 1992 Blackbirch Graphics, Inc.
First Edition

5 4 3 2 1

Created and produced in association with Blackbirch Graphics.
Series Editor: Bruce S. Glassman

Library of Congress Cataloging-in-Publication Data
Schleifer, Jay.
    Our Declaration of Independence / Jay Schleifer—1st ed.
    (I know America)
    Includes bibliographical references and index.
    Summary: A history of the Declaration of Independence, describing the
events leading up to it, the key players in its drafting, and the actual writing
and its adoption.
    ISBN 1-56294-205-0 (lib. bdg.)
    1. United States—Declaration of Independence. 2. United States—
Politics and government—Revolution, 1775–1783. [1. United States.
Declaration of Independence.] I. Title. II. Series.
E221.S33   1992
973.3'13—dc20   91-43229
                                                            CIP
                                                            AC

Acknowledgments and Photo Credits
Cover (text), p. 31: Smithsonian Institution; Cover (painting), pp. 32,
37: National Archives; Back cover, p. 26: University of Virginia;
pp. 4, 5: ©Stephen R. Brown/National Archives; pp. 6, 8, 9, 14, 22,
26, 31, 34, 39, 40: Library of Congress Collection; pp. 10, 13: North
Wind Picture Archives; pp. 11, 16, 17, 20, 33, 38: The National
Portrait Gallery, Smithsonian Institution; pp. 12, 24, 35: Culver
Pictures; p. 19: ©Sullivan/Virginia Department of Tourism; pp. 42,
44: AP/Wide World Photos.

Photo Research by **Inge King.**

CONTENTS

Young visitors crowd around the special display at the National Archives building in Washington, D.C.

The great National Archives building stands squarely at the center of Washington, D.C. From its broad steps you can see the white dome of the U.S. Capitol, where all our laws are made. The White House and the Supreme Court are just blocks away. And the building itself, made of the finest marble, looks made to last for centuries.

You climb the steps and enter the great central room. There's a large crowd of sightseers gathered, but their mood is quiet and respectful. Their attention is focused on a softly glowing glass showcase in the center of the room. The case is surrounded by guards twenty-four hours a day.

If you didn't know better, you'd wonder what all the fuss was about. Inside the case is what looks like a large sheet of yellowed paper (it's really parchment), covered with a hand-lettered message. The message, which seems to be oddly capitalized and punctuated, ends with dozens of scrawly signatures, many so faded they can no longer be read. The document is cracked and yellowed. It looks like something that should have been tossed away or recycled years ago.

You know why it wasn't. You're looking at the actual copy of the Declaration of Independence!

A Special Document

The Declaration was America's announcement to the world that we were no longer a colony of Great Britain but had become our own nation. It was our nation's "birth certificate," signed by some of the greatest Americans of all time: Thomas Jefferson, John Adams, Benjamin Franklin, and fifty-three others. Those are their actual signatures before you. You can almost see and hear the scratching of quill pens in their hands.

But there's so much more about the Declaration you can't see or hear. Blood flowed and anger raged in the battles that led up to the writing of it. Brilliant thoughts and powerful arguments surrounded it. A strange mix of fear and pride was felt by all involved in its creation.

All told, the story of the Declaration is an incredible one. It's a story you're about to learn.

The Declaration is housed in a unique vacuum-sealed case at the National Archives.

A NATION IN ALL BUT NAME

Many young people think that America began with the signing of the Declaration of Independence in July 1776. That's not quite right. America is much older. Many Native American peoples had inhabited the continent for thousands of years. And the first settlers from England arrived in 1607, over 150 years before the Declaration.

In a way, that's what caused the problem that led up to the Declaration. England was the "mother country." It had sent over, backed, and protected the first groups of English subjects who wanted to live in the "New World." These new settlements were called "colonies." They were owned by English subjects or by England and supposedly subject to English law.

Opposite:
Angry colonists burned copies of the Stamp Act in 1765 to protest unfair taxes imposed by Great Britain.

King George III and the parliament of England imposed the taxes that later inspired America's colonists to revolt.

But because they were an ocean away from England, they were pretty much left to run their own affairs.

In those 150 years, the colonies set up their own schools, businesses, postal services, as well as their own local governments. As a group, they learned to do all the things nations usually do. They formed a nation in all but name. After 150 years, the colonies had no further need of British rule.

The Unrest Begins

The real trouble began in the 1760s. England, which had joined with Wales and Scotland to become Great Britain, was always fighting wars with France. And the latest of these wars had just broken out in Europe. It would later be called the Seven Years' War.

A new feature this time was that both Britain and France now had colonies in America. The British colonies ran from what is now Maine down as far as Georgia. The French colonies were in Canada.

When the parent nations got a full-blown fight going in Europe, their colonies had their own smaller version of the war. Because the French enlisted the aid of local Native Americans against the British, the American version of the Seven Years' War became known as the French and Indian War.

When the war ended, Britain walked off with victory, giant chunks of Canada, and a huge bill to pay. The British expected their colonies in America to pay a big piece of that bill.

Problems with Taxes

Payment would come through various taxes set on the colonies by the British government. Britain always had the power to tax America, and some of the taxes had been around for years, but they had never really been collected. Now they would be.

Other taxes were new. One was a tax on every letter, newspaper, and government paper issued in the colonies. The tax was collected by selling a stamp that had to be put on the papers. It was therefore called the Stamp Act. During the dispute with the colonies that followed the Stamp Act, the British government charged taxes on various items shipped into the colonies. It also started meddling with the government of the colonies by setting new rules for trying cases that involved shipping.

Angry over taxes, townspeople punished many officials of the English government. Here, a crowd tars and feathers tax collector John Malcom.

In December 1773, a group of colonists led by Samuel Adams dressed up as Indians and dumped 342 chests of tea into Boston Harbor. This protest of the tax on tea came to be known as the Boston Tea Party.

Most Americans had no problem with paying taxes. They were British subjects and most were proud of it, and they understood that taxes were the cost of government. But they had a real problem with the way the taxes were placed on them. Cities and towns of England had representatives in the Parliament, the law-making body of the British government, giving them a voice in what tax laws were made. But the colonies had no representatives in the government. "No taxation without representation!" was the cry that was soon heard throughout the colonies.

A Tea Party in Boston Harbor

Sam Adams was one of the leading opponents of the Stamp Act. When the British finally repealed the act, they tried to pass other acts, such as a tax on various items, including tea. Adams again led the opposition. He got the merchants of Massachusetts to agree not to import anything from Britain on which there was a tax. He also drew up a letter, which the Massachusetts legislature sent to the law-making bodies of the other twelve colonies. This letter explained why the British actions were unjust, and asked for ideas on how the colonies could work together to oppose them. Other merchants joined in the refusal to import taxed goods, and the British backed off again, but kept the tax on tea. In 1772, Adams responded by suggesting that each town form a Committee of Correspondence. The members of the committee would write letters to the committees in other towns and colonies, letting them know what the British authorities were doing there, and how the colonials were fighting back.

But Sam Adams did not stop at words. When a shipment of tea arrived in Boston Harbor, the governor said the ships could not leave without paying the tea tax. Sam and his friends took action. Dressed as Indians, they rowed small boats into Boston Harbor, where several large cargo ships filled with tea were waiting to unload. On a moonless night in December 1773, they boarded the ships, whooped and hollered, and then dumped 342 chests of tea into the harbor—$90,000 worth! That night would always be known as the Boston Tea Party.

When word got to England, the government was furious. The Parliament immediately passed a string of punishing laws designed to teach Boston a lesson it would never forget! The harbor was closed to traffic—this deprived the city of food and other goods—and thousands of British soldiers streamed into town. The townspeople were forced to house the hated troops, (called "lobsterbacks" because of their red coats).

Samuel Adams was a strong colonial leader in the fight against unfair taxation by England.

The Colonies Band Together

What happened next completely surprised the British. The American colonies, which seldom cooperated on anything important, rose as one in support of Boston. The Committees of Correspondence told the other colonies about the trouble in Boston. And the other colonies responded. Colonists gave food, money, and other goods to Bostonians they had never even seen and didn't know—just because they were fellow Americans. The colonies—all but Georgia—also sent representatives to a meeting in Philadelphia. It was called the Congress, and is known today as the First Continental Congress. It met in September 1774, and drew up a list of grievances against the British. It also called on the colonies to boycott British goods and to form militias to defend their rights. Faced with such resistance, the British in time backed down.

John Adams, Robert Morris, Alexander Hamilton, and Thomas Jefferson were the leaders of the First Continental Congress. They met in 1774 to draw up a list of complaints against Britain.

Paul Revere made his famous midnight ride in April 1775 to warn colonists that British troops were on their way.

But a spark had been lit that would not die. And it was only a question of time before the spark flared to a flame. That happened in April 1775, again in Massachusetts. British officers learned that American patriots had stored arms in a small town near Boston. British troops moved out by night to surprise the Americans, get the guns, and arrest the "outlaws."

But as the British began to stir, American spies were watching. In a wild ride that lasted all night, Paul Revere and William Dawes raced through the countryside, alerting everyone that the Redcoats were coming. Large groups of armed Americans, called Minutemen (because they were ready at a minute's notice) gathered in towns along the way.

The Redcoats and patriots met at the tiny towns of Lexington and Concord. As the sun rose, blood ran. No one knows who fired the first shot—later called "the shot heard round the world." But it didn't much matter. Revolution and a bloody war between Mother England and her American "children" had finally come.

★ 2

THE FOUNDERS OF OUR NATION

While battles raged around Boston, another kind of war was going on within the hearts and minds of Americans everywhere. Although colonists were used to running their own affairs and making their own decisions, they were still British subjects and generally happy to be so. The British Empire was the greatest power on earth, and belonging to it was like being a member of the best club in town.

Rebels Against the Mother Country

Many Americans of the 1770s were ready to hate the Parliament or certain British leaders, but not the king. Not *their* king. For these reasons, many Americans

Opposite:
The Battle of Bunker Hill, in June 1775, was the first major battle of the Revolution.

John Adams was one of the first colonial leaders to say that the colonies should fight to become completely independent of Britain.

hoped to settle the argument with Britain, so that the "happy arrangement" between mother country and colonies could go on as before. All they wanted was their rights as British people, such as the right to be represented in Parliament, no more than that.

But here and there, a few did want more. Sam Adams was such a person, and so was his cousin John Adams, also of Massachusetts.

John was a forty-year-old lawyer who had held some offices and sat in the Massachusetts legislature, but whose real claim to fame was that he didn't want to settle peaceably with the king. Instead, Adams wanted to totally end America's ties with Britain. He wanted the colonies to join together and to form an entirely new nation!

Adams quickly became, as he himself said, "obnoxious and disliked." Often it seemed that only John's beloved wife, Abigail, could stand him at all on this issue. Nevertheless, there was power in John's ideas, and also in the force he used to present them.

The Second Continental Congress

In 1775, leaders in all the colonies decided to call another meeting, called the Second Continental Congress, to discuss what to do about the increasing problems. Each colony agreed to send representatives to the city of Philadelphia, where they would sit. Massachusetts decided to send the hotheaded rebel John Adams, among others.

Adams's opposite in the Congress was another man named John from the rich and powerful colony of Pennsylvania. Like many leaders and patriots of his area, John Dickinson was a landowner. His farm, outside Philadelphia, covered thousands of acres.

To many wealthy men like Dickinson, the battles of Boston were just something he read about in the newspapers. Few British troops had ever come to Pennsylvania, and none were expected. Dickinson generally favored the idea of America as someday becoming its own nation. But not now! Not yet! It would be years before the colonies would be ready to take on the greatest power on earth in a war!

When Dickinson thought of such a war, he became heartsick. At every chance he had, Dickinson spoke in favor of settling the quarrel with England so that peace could be restored.

A Man Named Franklin

Another man sent to Congress was named Benjamin Franklin. Although Franklin lived near Dickinson, he was light-years away from him in thought.

At age seventy, Franklin had enjoyed a rich and exciting life. He loved good ale, good jokes, and fun. He was a creative thinker, whose many brilliant inventions are still in use today. Among Franklin's innovations are the lightning rod, the Franklin stove, and bifocal eyeglasses, a pair of which he always wore on the tip of his nose.

Benjamin Franklin was a beloved American statesman for many years.

Hobbled by gout, a painful disease of the joints, Franklin rode around in a sedan chair. This was a common form of transportation in colonial days. Franklin's sedan chair was carried by four just-released convicts from the Philadelphia city prison.

Behind this fun-loving attitude, though, was a powerful mind. What Franklin wanted, almost as strongly as John Adams, was a free and independent America. As the only member of the Pennsylvania group to strongly favor independence, Franklin was an important answering voice to Dickinson.

The Voice of Jefferson

As Congress assembled in 1775, and sat on into 1776, one other important voice was about to be heard—though more through the written word than the spoken. Young Thomas Jefferson, all of thirty-three years old, had just been appointed to the Congress, representing Virginia.

Jefferson, a brilliant man and a wealthy Virginia landowner, knew all about the problems with Britain. But his main interest was far deeper than what new tax laws were passed or what battles were to be fought. Jefferson questioned the whole idea of government power, where it came from, who had the right to use it, and who had the right to change its use. These were questions that could topple the whole world, as people then knew it; questions that could bring down kings like so many chess pieces, in nations all over the

BESIDES WRITING THE DECLARATION

Thomas Jefferson had talents without end. Besides writing the Declaration, he also...

★ Was a brilliant lawyer.

★ Was a scientist. Because he took readings, we know the temperature and weather while the Declaration was debated. At 9 a.m. on July 4, 1776, it was 72 degrees Fahrenheit.

★ Was an architect. He designed several buildings, including his own home at Monticello, in Charlottesville, Virginia.

★ Was an inventor. He created a portable desk for work on the Declaration, and, some say, invented the rocking chair.

★ Spoke several languages.

★ Was an artist and musician. He played the violin, three hours a day when at home.

★ Founded the University of Virginia.

★ Died on July 4, 1826, the *exact* fiftieth anniversary of the Declaration. (John Adams died the very same day.)

Monticello

world. In the end, the answers Jefferson and others found to those questions did just that!

Adams, Dickinson, Franklin, and Jefferson— these were the major players in the drama that led to the Declaration. But there were others not playing starring roles. There were fifty other representatives in Congress. There were thousands of soldiers on all sides fighting the war for independence. More than 10 million people would, in the end, be affected— 2.5 million Americans, and 8 million British.

3

"THESE UNITED COLONIES ARE AND . . . OUGHT TO BE FREE . . ."

The Congress, which first met to decide what to do about the war with Britain, had by 1776 begun to be at the center of that war. Each day's mail brought new reports from the war, many from General Washington himself, most not very encouraging. By the summer, American troops had been fighting for more than a year, and losing a lot of the time. That was no surprise. The American army was mostly made up of farm boys, led by a few veterans of the French and Indian War.

The way things were set up, Congress had to ask the colonies to provide guns, money, uniforms, and whatever else was needed. But what was then provided was up to the colonies. Congress had no way to force them to supply a single musket ball.

Opposite: Members of the Second Continental Congress met in Philadelphia in 1775. After long debates that went on for months, the Congress voted to become independent of Britain.

As one might expect, there was never enough of anything. Most soldiers didn't even have proper uniforms, some not even shoes. Washington spent as much time begging as he did fighting. This ragtag bunch was expected to defeat the greatest military power on earth!

The Colonial Advantage

There were bright spots. While colonial soldiers couldn't march to save themselves, they could shoot well. Many depended for food on the ability to drop a running squirrel at a hundred yards. A Redcoat was a lot larger and a lot slower than a squirrel. And the Redcoats wore uniforms with bright white belts that crisscrossed on their chests. The point at which their belts crossed made a deadly target to aim at.

Then too, because American troops knew almost nothing about the usual rules of battle, they invented a way to fight that the British had never before run into.

Normal European battle rules called for the armies to march at each other in straight lines and fire openly. The line with the most soldiers left standing at the end of the battle won.

The colonials refused to march. Instead, they fired from behind walls and trees, hitting and running before the British could fire back. The British felt this tactic wasn't "civilized." But it was effective.

But the troops also had the troublesome habit of going home after each battle. There was planting to be done, after all. And because each army was under local government control, there was little Congress could do about it.

Still, the colonials were starting to feel they had a chance, even if a slim one. That fired up the debate over what the war was really about. Should it just be to get from Britain the rights the British living there had—the Dickinson view? Or should America go "all the way" to independence, as John Adams insisted in his most ungracious and insulting way?

The Impact of *Common Sense*

In January 1776, something else happened to add to the debate. A newly arrived Englishman named Thomas Paine sat at his writing table and composed a little book called *Common Sense*. Paine had held a dozen jobs and had never been successful at anything, but his book brought him fame for all time. In it, he laid out the simple reasons why America *had* to be

The first pages of Thomas Paine's *Common Sense,* which explained why America had to be free of Britain.

independent, in language anyone could understand. How could a tiny island nation, three thousand miles away, run a great continent, Paine asked? Ridiculous! Independence was just "common sense!"

Nobody kept best-seller lists then, but if anyone had, *Common Sense* would have set sales records. In ninety days, it sold 120,000 copies. That would be like selling 13 million copies today!

Five months later, leaders in Virginia forced Congress to deal with the issue officially. The Virginians passed a decree saying that, in their view, "these United Colonies are, and of right ought to be, free and independent States." One of Virginia's leaders, Richard Henry Lee, carried this message to Congress and, on June 7, he asked officially that it be voted on, once and for all, yea or nay.

Yearning for Independence

If the vote had been taken on that day, the answer would have been divided. In favor of independence, of course, was Massachusetts. But the rest of New England—New Hampshire, Connecticut, and Rhode Island—was also in agreement. (Maine and Vermont were formed later.)

Georgia was also in favor of independence. Maryland looked as if it would agree. But Delaware was split down the middle, and New York couldn't seem to decide. In fact, its delegates just sat most votes out. New Jersey, North Carolina, and South Carolina were question marks.

Of Pennsylvania, there was no question. Only Franklin was for independence. Dickinson was against it to the death, and his views influenced the other members of the group. Pennsylvania was as solid a nay as there could be.

At that early date, seven of thirteen colonies already favored independence, with some of the other five colonies sure to join. John Adams and his friends knew they had a sure majority to win, but as they talked, they realized that a majority win would not do. If any colony did not agree to independence, Britain could drive a massive hole through the new nation by simply joining with that colony. It was all or nothing, and with Pennsylvania out of reach, it seemed, so was independence.

Adams and other leaders made two decisions: They would have the vote on Virginia's idea put off for three weeks. During that time, they would work to turn the undecided colonies to independence and hope for a miracle with Pennsylvania.

Second, just in case they could actually get independence passed, they would write up a special document to declare to the world why America had broken free—a "Declaration of Independence."

★ 4

"YOU DO IT!"

To get the Declaration written, Congress created a small committee: John Adams led it, assisted by Benjamin Franklin, Roger Sherman of Connecticut, and a New York delegate, Robert Livingston. They also added one other member who had a reputation as a good writer, Thomas Jefferson of Virginia.

The Declaration Committee went to work, and quickly realized that someone had to put the thing on paper. Franklin said his writing was too full of clever lines and jokes—not the style for the job—and that he was too old to change his style now! Sherman and Livingston begged off, saying they had neither talent nor time. That left Adams and Jefferson, and one of the most amazing discussions ever captured in history:

Opposite:
Thomas Jefferson was responsible for drafting the first version of the Declaration in 1776.

27

Jefferson: You do it!

Adams: I will not. You should do it!

Jefferson: Oh no! Why will you not? You ought to do it!

Adams: I will not.

Jefferson: Why?

Adams: Reasons enough.

Jefferson: What can be your reasons?

Adams: Reason first: You are a Virginian and a Virginian should be at the head of this business. Reason second: I am obnoxious, suspected, and unpopular. You are very much otherwise. Reason third: You can write ten times better than I can.

Jefferson: Well, if you are decided, I will do as well as I can.

A Declaration Is Written

For the next two weeks, the candles burned late in Jefferson's rented room at the home of a Philadelphia bricklayer. Jefferson wrote and rewrote, and his scribbles, cross-outs, and write-ins show the furious speed at which his mind was working. For the Declaration, he reached back into everything he had ever read about government and its proper place in the world—and he had read a lot!

Jefferson was following a whole new idea: that governments belonged to the people, and that kings, if they existed at all, should serve the people, not simply rule them. Until that time, only a few brave thinkers had even written about such ideas. Nobody had ever tried building a nation around them.

On June 28, several closely spaced pages of writing appeared on the desk of the clerk of the Congress. The American idea of independence had finally been spelled out on paper.

What Mr. Jefferson Hath Written

Jefferson's Declaration had three parts. The first gave the reasons America thought it had a right to be independent. The second was a long, long list of evil deeds Britain had done to America—it was by far the most popular part of the paper at the time. The final part noted that as far as America was concerned, it was now a free and independent nation, and that the new nation would break free of Britain and take its rightful place as a power in the world.

What's more, Jefferson wrote that the Declaration had come from something called "the united States of America." It was the first time anyone had ever called the colonies by such a name.

You can read the text of the Declaration on page 45, but we'd like to take the time to look at some parts of it now, and discuss what they mean.

When in the Course of human events, it becomes necessary for one people to dissolve the political bands which have connected

THE GLOSSARY OF INDEPENDENCE

The following are explanations for some important terms and ideas that are used in the Declaration of Independence:

self-evident—true without needing proof.

unalienable rights—rights that cannot be taken away.

usurpations—the theft of people's rights.

tyranny—the use of government power to do evil.

absolved—released from.

allegiance—loyalty.

Divine Providence—help from heaven.

them with another, and to assume among the powers of the earth, the separate and equal station to which the Laws of Nature and of Nature's God entitle them, a decent respect to the opinions of mankind required that they should declare the causes which impel them to the separation.

In this section, Jefferson was saying that when a new nation is born by separating itself from another, it's just simple respect to explain to the world why that happened.

We hold these truths to be self-evident, that all men are created equal, that they are endowed by their Creator with certain unalienable Rights, that among these are Life, Liberty and the pursuit of Happiness. That to secure these rights, Governments are instituted among Men, deriving their just powers from the consent of the governed,—That whenever any Form of Government becomes destructive of these ends, it is the Right of the People to alter or to abolish it....

This section starts with the simple phrase, "We hold these truths to be self-evident." That one really turned things upside down. It was just the truth, and that was that. The door was shut on argument. This is the most important part of the Declaration, by far. In it, Jefferson states that all people are created equal, and that all have the right to life, freedom, and the chance to do well in life—the pursuit of happiness. He says that government is formed to protect these rights, and when the government starts to get in the way of these rights, the people can change their government.

For 1776, this was an incredible string of ideas! For one thing, almost nobody felt then that all people were created equal. It was taken for granted that

The Declaration of Independence in its final handwritten version.

kings, and sometimes nobles, were born better than ordinary, common people. They were born with special rights no one else could have.

Jefferson's statement that government belonged to the people shook their beliefs. The leaders of the time ruled the people, they didn't work *for* them. What's more, no one had the right to overthrow a government, no matter how great its sins. If anyone tried, that person was often punished by death.

Jefferson is clear about the people's right to overthrow a bad government. He even says it is the duty of the people to overthrow an unfair government.

In the next section, Jefferson listed twenty-seven ways in which the king had deprived America of its liberty. These ranged from refusing to let important laws be passed to the charge that he had "plundered our seas, ravaged our Coasts, burnt our towns, and destroyed the lives of our people."

In conclusion, Jefferson said that the "good People of these Colonies," using the right to overthrow a bad government, were now publishing and declaring that they had broken free of Britain, and would now do all the things real nations do. These included waging war, making peace, setting up commerce, and other actions. He also stated that, in support of this Declaration, all in Congress agreed to "pledge to each other our Lives, our Fortunes and our sacred Honor."

The Congress debated the ideas of independence in the Philadelphia statehouse.

The Vote

Although the Declaration was now drafted, there was no guarantee it would ever see a printing press. First would come the all-important vote on independence.

On July 1, as it had planned, Congress began to discuss the matter. It was a blustery, stormy day, and the mood of the delegates matched the weather. After some routine business, John Dickinson got up and began to speak. Adams and his supporters ducked for cover. They knew that their favorite idea was about to get blasted with both barrels.

The Argument Against Independence

Dickinson had carefully prepared for this moment, knowing that his views had fewer supporters and that if Pennsylvania were the only holdout, his colony might be forced to vote yea. He spoke passionately for hours, carefully tearing apart Mr. Adams's dream point by point.

"Independence," cried Dickinson, "is like destroying our house in winter before we build another shelter." He predicted that American cities would burn, that Britain would join with the Indian tribes, supporting them in a vicious attack. "Scalping parties will whoop along New York's Wall Street and Philadelphia's Market Street," Dickinson shouted, knowing well that this argument would hit home. Many Americans viewed the native tribes as "savages" capable of unspeakably evil acts.

John Dickinson was one of the most powerful and vocal leaders against independence.

A DECLARATION TIMELINE

The Boston Massacre

Here are some of the most important events that led up to the Declaration of Independence, and when they happened:

1760: George III becomes King of England.

1763–1766: Stamp Act passed to raise money from the colonies. Colonists riot in protest, and form a Congress to decide what to do. Act is repealed.

1767–1769: More laws and rules put upon the colonists.

1770: British troops argue with and fire on colonials in the streets of Boston, killing several—the "Boston Massacre."

1773–1774: Parliament passes the Tea Act, leading to the Boston Tea Party. Britain fights back by closing the port of Boston.

1775: The Revolution begins at Lexington in April, followed by the Battle of Bunker Hill. There's more and more fighting in more and more places.

1776: *Common Sense* is published. In May, Virginia asks Congress to decide on independence, and in July, the new nation called the United States is born.

Unfortunately, no one has recorded how Adams responded to Dickinson. But Jefferson remembered that the words came "with a power that moved us from our seats."

Then came one of those happy events that occur just by chance. New Jersey had been undecided for some time, but a new group of representatives was supposed to show up at any moment with some new instructions from home. As Adams thundered to a close, these gentlemen suddenly popped in from the rain. Their new instructions were to vote yea.

Sensing victory, Adams quickly called for a vote. The result was favorable, but far from what he needed. Pennsylvania and South Carolina voted nay. New York did not vote, as it had not received orders from home. And Delaware also did not vote. One of its three delegates was not present, and the other two were split. Their votes cancelled out.

The Missing Delegate

The missing delegate was Caesar Rodney, a forty-seven-year-old farmer known to be in favor of independence. He was at home some eighty miles away doing local business, and he was sick with a cancer that eventually killed him. Rodney lived in constant pain, and few wanted to bother him.

Nevertheless, the yea group realized that he would be needed to swing Delaware to their side. A messenger was hired and a note was written to Rodney. The horseman raced off into the storm. He arrived at Rodney's farmhouse after midnight.

Opening the door in his nightshirt, Rodney quickly read the message and knew at once what he had to do. Despite the howling gale, he immediately saddled up and left for Philadelphia.

On July 2, the doors of Congress flew open to reveal an almost unrecognizable Caesar Rodney,

Caesar Rodney of Delaware provided a key vote for independence in the Congress.

dripping water and mud on the fine wooden floor, and still wearing his spurs. "Delaware votes yea," he said, exhausted and out of breath.

During that day's vote, South Carolina also voted yea. The delegates had thought about it and decided to go along with independence. With New York still not voting, it all came down to Pennsylvania.

A Miracle in Pennsylvania

When all the delegates arrived on the morning of July 2, 1776, John Dickinson was not in his usual place. Everyone sensed that something incredible had happened the night before—a miracle in Pennsylvania.

The miracle was Benjamin Franklin. He had put all his skills to work on the other Pennsylvanians. And by the time he was done, John Dickinson was heavily outnumbered. When the clerk called for the vote of Pennsylvania, Franklin said simply, "Pennsylvania votes yea." Weeks later New York received approval to vote yea, making the vote 13-0.

It was done. America had broken free of Britain. The United States of America had been born!

Changes to the Declaration

With independence now declared, Congress took aim at Jefferson's Declaration. No sooner had the clerk finished reading it than the changes began—dozens of them. Many were just for language; Jefferson was not happy with the changes. He sat frowning as the delegates picked his work apart.

The Question of Slavery

Then delegates from the South arose with a change more serious than the rest. Jefferson had included in the list of the king's misdeeds that he had "waged war against...a distant people, carrying them into slavery." By this, of course, he meant the black slaves of the South, stolen by force from Africa.

The South wanted this out. Southern delegates refused to sign the document if this item remained. They might even withdraw their support from the war.

Jefferson, a wealthy slave owner who had already promised to free his family's fifty slaves, had hoped freedom for America would mean freedom for its half million blacks—one of every five people in the nation. This was not to be. The lines were crossed out. But the problem of slavery was not to be erased that easily. Eighty-five years later, Americans would fight the Civil War in part because of this major error at the birth of the nation.

With all changes made, Congress now voted to accept the Declaration. There was nothing left to do but sign and print it.

That night, the scribbled-over Declaration, with all the changes, went to the print shop of John Dunlap of Philadelphia. The date at the top was the date of signature, July 4, 1776. Later a beautiful hand-lettered parchment copy was made for signing by all the delegates of the Congress. And on August 2, they signed, including a few delegates who had never voted on it.

The Declaration was cheered across the nation when it was first read to citizens of the colonies.

37

Within days, copies of the Declaration were read far and wide. Jefferson's ringing words were a sensation. Crowds cheered and cheered, and some did more than that. When the Declaration was read to Washington's troops, they turned into a mob and tore down a statue of King George.

Read Across the Atlantic

The Declaration had another effect. Reading it in Europe, other nations now felt it would be legal to offer help to the brand-new United States. They had been unwilling to help America so long as it was a part of Britain. France soon offered ships and money, which helped to turn the tide of war.

WHO WERE THE SIGNERS?

The fifty-six signers of the Declaration came from all walks of life. Here are some facts about them:

★ Forty-eight were born in America, eight overseas.

★ Twenty-two were college graduates.

★ The occupations of the signers were varied:

fifteen were businessmen, twelve were farmers or landowners; one was a minister, and twenty-three were lawyers!

★ The youngest signer, Edward Rutledge of South Carolina, was twenty-six; the oldest, Benjamin Franklin, was seventy.

John Hancock

The Influence of the Declaration

Finally, there is the fate of the ideas behind the Declaration. These timeless truths about equality and fair government have gone on to inspire other nations to build their versions of freedom, even today. In the 1980s and early 1990s, many Eastern European nations and what later became the Commonwealth of Independent States worked hard to build their versions of freedom and democracy.

But what of the Declaration itself—the famous piece of parchment signed on August 2, 1776, by the members of Congress? Now *that's* a story in itself.

The first approved version of the Declaration of Independence was signed on July 4, 1776. Later, on August 2, a neatly written final version was presented to the delegates for their signatures.

CHAPTER

5

THE PARCHMENT TRAIL

You might think that the birth certificate of the United States would be kept in a safe place, to be treasured, protected, and watched over. Was it? Yes and no.

After the signing, the parchment was simply rolled up and kept with the other papers of Congress. Later in the war as the British closed in on Philadelphia, Congress moved on to Baltimore. They took the Declaration with them. It was tossed on a wagon with supply lists, meeting minutes, and other papers.

The First President

In 1789, George Washington was officially sworn in as America's first president, and received the Declaration into his care. He chose to give it to his secretary of

Opposite:
George Washington became America's first president in 1789 and was given official possession of the Declaration.

In 1976, bicentennial celebrations spanned the nation and often lasted for months. Among the many festivities were ceremonies to honor the 200th birthday of the Declaration.

state—Thomas Jefferson. Many wonder how he felt seeing it again!

When the government moved to its new capital city of Washington, D.C., the Declaration went along. And when Washington was attacked by the British in the War of 1812, the famous parchment was in terrible danger of being destroyed. In this dreadful moment, someone had the sense to stuff it, along with other papers, in a cloth bag and throw the bag into a wagon. The driver hid America's most famous document in an ordinary barn overnight, and then took it to the house of a clergyman nearby.

When the danger had passed, the parchment was returned to Washington to be kept at the Treasury Department. Soon after, someone decided to make a special copy of the Declaration by sprinkling it with chemicals that were to cause the image to be reproduced on another paper. It was not a wise move! The chemicals damaged the ink, and many signatures faded. After that, the document got a few years' rest.

When the new Patent Office building was completed, someone decided this fine new structure was a dandy place to display the Declaration. Placed in an ordinary frame, it was nailed to a wall and left there for more than twenty years!

The Document Fades

When someone finally removed the Declaration from the wall to be displayed on its hundreth birthday—July 4, 1876—at a great fair in Philadelphia, the historic parchment was yellowed and cracked, and some of it was almost unreadable.

By the 1920s, a better solution was found. A special case was built at the Library of Congress that allowed the public to view the famous parchment while, at the same time, it remained protected. This was to be the Declaration's resting place.

When America entered World War II in 1941, there were great fears that enemy agents might strike at this beloved symbol of America, perhaps bombing the Library of Congress or trying to break the case. For protection, the Declaration was secretly removed from the Library and taken under armed guard to the safest place anyone could think of—the underground gold vault at Fort Knox, Kentucky. There, surrounded by tons of steel and stone, and more than 40,000 soldiers, it remained until the war's end, when it was returned to the Library.

A National Archives Is Built

There was one more short trip in the Declaration's future. In the 1920s, the government had decided to build a National Archives to house the nation's most important papers. A special exhibit case was created for the Declaration, one that looks like a large glass

Today, the Declaration of Independence still inspires young Americans to take pride in their country and to enjoy the freedoms that America offers.

showcase but in fact is a protective device. The case holding the parchment is sealed against air pollution, and the glass has special filters to keep out damaging light. Each night, the Declaration is safely locked up. And should there ever be an attack on Washington— even a nuclear attack—the Declaration can be lowered in seconds on a special elevator into a bombproof shelter. The Constitution, which is also stored there, has the same protection.

According to officials, nothing will ever again harm either of America's founding documents.

This book began in the central room of the National Archives and there it ends. But the road to freedom opened by the Declaration of Independence will most likely go on forever.

THE DECLARATION OF INDEPENDENCE

In Congress, July 4, 1776

The unanimous Declaration of the thirteen united States of America

When in the Course of human events, it becomes necessary for one people to dissolve the political bands which have connected them with another, and to assume among the powers of the earth, the separate and equal station to which the Laws of Nature and of Nature's God entitle them, a decent respect to the opinions of mankind requires that they should declare the causes which impel them to the separation.

We hold these truths to be self-evident, that all men are created equal, that they are endowed by their Creator with certain unalienable Rights, that among these are Life, Liberty and the pursuit of Happiness. That to secure these rights, Governments are instituted among Men, deriving their just powers from the consent of the governed,—That whenever any Form of Government becomes destructive of these ends, it is the Right of the People to alter or to abolish it, and to institute new Government, laying its foundation on such principles and organizing its power in such form, as to them shall seem most likely to effect their Safety and Happiness. Prudence, indeed, will dictate that Governments long established should not be changed for light and transient causes; and accordingly all experience hath shewn, that mankind are more disposed to suffer, while evils are sufferable, than to right themselves by abolishing the forms to which they are accustomed. But when a long train of abuses and usurpations, pursuing invariably the same Object evinces a design to reduce them under absolute Despotism, it is their right, it is their duty, to throw off such Government, and to provide new Guards for their future security.—Such has been the patient sufferance of these Colonies; and such is now the necessity which constrains them to alter their former Systems of Government. The history of the present King of Great Britain is a history of repeated injuries and usurpations, all having in direct object the establishment of an absolute Tyranny over these States. To prove this, let Facts be submitted to a candid world.

He has refused his Assent to Laws, the most wholesome and necessary for the public good.

He has forbidden his Governors to pass Laws of immediate and pressing importance, unless suspended in their operation till his Assent should be obtained; and when so suspended, he has utterly neglected to attend to them.

He has refused to pass other Laws for the accommodation of large districts of people, unless those people would relinquish the right of Representation in the Legislature, a right ines- timable to them and formidable to tyrants only.

He has called together legislative bodies at places unusual, uncomfortable, and distant from the depository of their public Records, for the sole purpose of fatiguing them into compliance with his measures.

He has dissolved Representative Houses repeatedly, for opposing with manly firmness his invasions on the rights of the people.

He has refused for a long time, after such dissolutions, to cause others to be elected; whereby the Legislative powers, incapable of Annihilation, have returned to the People at large for their exercise; the State remaining in the mean time exposed to all the dangers of invasion from without, and convulsions within.

He has endeavoured to prevent the population of these States; for that purpose obstructing the Laws for Naturalization of Foreigners; refusing to pass others to encourage their migrations hither, and raising the conditions of new Appropriations of Lands.

He has obstructed the Administration of Justice, by refusing his Assent to Laws for establishing Judiciary powers.

He has made Judges dependent on his Will alone, for the tenure of their offices, and the amount and payment of their salaries.

He has erected a multitude of New Offices, and sent hither swarms of Officers to harass our people, and eat out their substance.

He has kept among us, in times of peace, Standing Armies without the Consent of our legislatures.

He has affected to render the Military independent of and superior to the Civil power.

He has combined with others to subject us to a jurisdiction foreign to our constitution, and acknowledged by our laws; giving his Assent to their Acts of pretended Legislation:

For quartering large bodies of armed troops among us:

For protecting them, by a mock Trial, from punishment for any Murders which they should commit on the inhabitants of these States:

For cutting off our Trade with all parts of the world:

For imposing Taxes on us without our Consent:

For depriving us in many cases, of the benefits of Trial by Jury:

For transporting us beyond Seas to be tried for pretended offenses:

For abolishing the free System of English Laws in a neighbouring Province, establishing therein an Arbitrary government, and enlarging its Boundaries so as to render it at once an example and fit instrument for introducing the same absolute rule into these Colonies:

For taking away our Charters, abolishing our most valuable Laws, and altering fundamentally the Forms of our Governments:

For suspending our own Legislatures, and declaring themselves invested with power to legislate for us in all cases whatsoever.

He has abdicated Government here, by declaring us out of his Protection and waging War against us.

He has plundered our seas, ravaged our Coasts, burnt our towns, and destroyed the lives of our people.

He is at this time transporting large Armies of foreign Mercenaries to compleat the works of death, desolation and tyranny, already begun with circumstances of Cruelty and perfidy scarcely paralleled in the most barbarous ages, and totally unworthy the Head of a civilized nation.

He has constrained our fellow Citizens taken Captive on the high Seas to bear Arms against their Country, to become the executioners of their friends and Brethren, or to fall themselves by their Hands.

He has excited domestic insurrections amongst us, and had endeavoured to bring on the inhabitants of our frontiers, the merciless Indian Savages, whose known rule of warfare is an undistinguished destruction of all ages, sexes and conditions.

In every stage of these Oppressions We have Petitioned for Redress in the most humble terms: Our repeated Petitions have been answered only by repeated injury. A Prince, whose character is thus marked by every act which may define a Tyrant, is unfit to be the ruler of a free people.

Nor have We been wanting in attentions to our British brethren. We have warned them from time to time of attempts by their legislature to extend an unwarrantable jurisdiction over us. We have reminded them of the circumstances of our emigration and settlement here. We have appealed to their native justice and magna-nimity, and we have conjured them by the ties of our common kindred to disavow these usurpations, which, would inevitably interrupt our connections and correspondence. They too have been deaf to the voice of justice and of consanguinity. We must, therefore, acquiesce in the necessity, which denounces our Separation, and hold them, as we hold the rest of mankind, Enemies in War, in Peace Friends.

We, therefore, the Representatives of the united States of America, in General Congress, Assembled, appealing to the Supreme Judge of the world for the rectitude of our intentions, do, in the Name, and by Authority of the good

People of these Colonies, solemnly publish and declare, That these United Colonies are, and of Right ought to be Free and Independent States; that they are Absolved from all Allegiance to the British Crown, and that all political connection between them and the State of Great Britain, is and ought to be totally dissolved; and that as Free and Independent States, they have full Power to levy War, conclude Peace, contract Alliances, establish Commerce, and to do all other Acts and Things which Independent States may of right do.

And for the support of this Declaration, with a firm reliance on the protection of Divine Providence, we mutually pledge to each other our Lives, our Fortunes and our sacred Honor.

New Hampshire
Josiah Bartlett
Wm. Whipple
Matthew Thornton

Massachusetts Bay
John Hancock
Sam Adams
John Adams
Robt Treat Paine
Elbridge Gerry

Rhode Island
Step. Hopkins
William Ellery

Connecticut
Roger Sherman
Sam Huntington
Wm. Williams
Oliver Wolcott

New York
Wm. Floyd
Phil. Livingston
Frans. Lewis
Lewis Morris

New Jersey
Richd. Stockton
Jno Witherspoon
Fras. Hopkinson
John Hart
Abra Clark

Pennsylvania
Robt Morris
Benjamin Rush
Benja. Franklin
John Morton
Geo. Clymer
Jas. Smith
Geo. Taylor
James Wilson
Geo. Ross

Delaware
Caesar Rodney
Geo Read
Tho M'Kean

Maryland
Samuel Chase
Wm. Paca
Thos. Stone
Charles Carroll of
    Carrollton

Virginia
George Wythe
Richard Henry Lee
Th Jefferson
Benja. Harrison
Thos. Nelson Jr.
Francis Lightfoot Lee
Carter Braxton

North Carolina
Wm Hooper
Joseph Hewes
John Penn

South Carolina
Edward Rutledge
Thos. Heyward Junr.
Thomas Lynch Junr.
Arthur Middleton

Georgia
Button Gwinnett
Lyman Hall
Geo Walton

For Further Reading

Commanger, Henry Steele, Editor. *The Great Declaration: A Book for Young Americans.* Indianapolis: The Bobbs-Merrill Company, 1958.

Feldman, Eve B. *Benjamin Franklin.* New York: Franklin Watts, 1990.

Hargrove, James. *Thomas Jefferson.* Chicago: Childrens Press, 1990.

Richards, N. *The Declaration of Independence.* Chicago: Childrens Press, 1990.

Ross, George E. *Know Your Declaration of Independence.* Chicago: Rand McNally & Company, 1963.

Index